UNDERSTORY

ALSO BY REBECCA ROTERT

Last Night at the Blue Angel

All the Animals We Ever Were

UNDERSTORY

A POEM

Rebecca Rotert

2020

Copyright © 2020 by Rebecca Rotert
All rights reserved.
Printed in the United States of America

Brighthorse Books
13202 North River Drive
Omaha, NE 68112

ISBN: 978-1-944467-22-7

Brighthorse Books is a small publisher of poetry, short fiction, and novels based in Omaha, Nebraska. For information about Brighthorse Books, visit us on the web at brighthorsebooks.com. For information about the Brighthorse Book Awards, go to https://brighthorsebooks.submittable.com/submit.

Brighthorse books are distributed to the trade through Ingram Book Group and its distribution partners. For more information, go to https://ipage.ingramcontent.com/ipage/li001.jsp.

UNDERSTORY

1.
It's as though
all you've known to be you
is a dry field by a ribboning river
near a town with a diner
and a Sinclair.

Until one day a million birds descend on you,
eat the hard seeds of your more regrettable hours,
nuzzle and purr in your dusty, wing-beat hair.

2.
For a million years they've come here,
the Sandhill Cranes.
Oldest species of bird
on earth, thousands
of gray ghosts
pecking their way through the stalk stumps
and cobs.

It was their song, if one
could call it that—
that rattle trapped
in a skin drum or
snake
in the belly of a turtle dove—
that lit us up, one cold weekend
in March.

Before the cranes,
I didn't know that I heard my heart
as no more than a murmur deep
in a distant, feathered body.

Belly-down on the side of a ditch,
we spied on them. An apparition
of a tribe. Gravel pressed
into our forearms.
The question in that ditch
soon to become the question of us:

How close can you get
to a vision
before it startles,
lifts into the sky
like it was never here?

3.
Come night, the cranes settle in shallow waters.
We're close enough to hear
the rumble in this one's throat.
She stands on one leg and tucks the other.
Beak under shoulder.
She looks like a mailbox.
Her red forehead the flag
signaling something inside,
a letter of desire
longing to be read.

600,000 mailboxes.

This larger one, sleepless,
wanders gingerly among the bodies,
his bustle of long hindfeathers ruffle
faintly as the hem of a nightgown
in a low lit hall.
We too rise and wander now.
Searching for the truck in the inky light.

4.
In the cab of the truck heading home,
our own primordial silence.
Objects in mirror are closer than they appear.

Nearer to town now the pink helmet of city light
presses into the sky. Inside it, our lives. But here
in this margin between who we are
and who we're about to become,
our arms touch.
Killdeer with their black beaks and black chokers beat the air
of a dry valley.
The remains of last season's death
beckon. Larvae, waste grain, centipedes, beetles. Snails
sucking themselves free of the warming ground.
We can't watch them circle and dive all night.
We do.

5.
I enter a dark house alone.
A lonely relief I repeat for years.
Here is my yellow couch, a crumbling hearth;
here the cat sleeps on a flannel I left on the floor.
Everything is as it was, and will go back to sleep,
except for me.

6.
Some nights are so long, rough,
they abrade every layer between you
and the velocity of time,
your bad ideas,
what you might have done
and might still do.
All the three a.m.
sentencings.

But just as you bow your head to your dark fate,
first light reaches through the east window,
her navy fingers, her white nails,
replaces every last protection,
if not in order.

I sit at the small kitchen table
with brown toast, cowboy coffee.
A warm, windows-open Sunday.
Pete and Ruthie, 5 and 9,
play in the yard next door.
He refuses some kind of directive and she
huffs into the house.

I lay down my hands. Listen to the new silence
in the yard.
Slowly, Pete begins to pull the milkweed pods,
dead a season, from the clutch of the chainlink fence.
He pries open one dry, stiff pod and is stunned,
half in English, half in Spanish,
by its shining flare of white silk.
He opens them all
like there's been some kind of mistake.

I keep still. Not so much to spy as to quiet the endless noise
of myself. So that Pete might know this moment alone—
the complicating surprise of beauty,
the way a dead thing can hold a living thing
until something stronger comes along.
A small boy in a strange, mean country, say.
A storm.

7.
I think to witness this from my window
will somehow keep his wonder alive. He will need it, I think.
I think many things that are wide of the mark.
But surely to witness is to respect
how crushed together our wonder and confusion
has been and always is?
Despite the fences.

Pete ushers the silks into his palm now.
He offers us all to the wind.

8.
Can you lie down
in the poem of your life
every day
and let it have you?

9.
There is no spectacle
to enrapture me this morning—
only the buckeye,
still without flowers or leaves,
naked gray muscle of trunk.

Do her ornaments and fruit, which is also to say, her poisons,
hum in the cambium?
That slippery vein
below the bark?
The darkness that nourishes and pumps like a heart.

Might I keep my more dangerous self held
under the skin of my stiffer self?
Does my answer matter?
These selves adhere to a clock
I didn't set.
I touch the buckeye's bark.
What can't be seen can be felt.
This quake.
Indistinguishable from my pulse.

How long before she fruits?
Those shiny brown bulbs like the eyes of deer,
smooth walnuts, like chocolates.
Pure poison, if opened.
If opened.

10.
The buckeye
is alive after all.
Plump buds the color of caramel
swell on the tips of the branches.
I see them now
when I look as I imagine you would look—
closely, long.

She will bloom in a matter
of weeks.
No one will witness
that first single thin petal
undressing itself
in the light.

That you are there,
somewhere,
that once I lay with you
before the altar of organisms,
saw them through the particular translations
of your mind and eyes,
changes me.
Shows me this
my life.

11.
This small, hot house.
Creaky. Ceiling plaster hangs here and there
in empty pages, seducing me,
same as the empty page before me
on this gray formica table.
Handle me.
Do something with me, please.
Anything.

It is maybe an art
to be in the uncertainty of your life
even as it doesn't look like a world
anyone else would build.
Can I imagine fashioning the days
from nerve and desire and weirdness alone,
the rooms of my mind
unadorned by the chipped ornaments
of hope?

12.
Mother said when I moved in here:
You must touch every surface of that house.
Every last baseboard, hinge.
Clean it or paint it I don't care.
Whatever you must do to make it yours,
to replace the spectres of then
with the facts of now.

13.
I press my fingers into the dark corner
of a small closet
where the smell of another woman,
years dead,
lingers still.

14.
Consuming the small but entire front lawn—
this linden. It shields me from the view to the south,
and from its view of me.
It's also called a bee tree but I won't know this
until the day you turn up here,
take me by the shoulder, stop me,
say, smell that.
Sweet. A bitter edge. Humming with buzz.
Between us then was only
the honeyed air,
deep shade,
the hungry batter
of frail, transparent wings.

15.
Behind the house, in a small square frame of chainlink,
patches of crabgrass,
an army of weeds demanding back their land,
and the solitary buckeye.

Overstory cannot thrive without understory.
The larger organisms, this buckeye, say,
require the company of other organisms to be well,
to not die slowly in a mute strangulation of grass.

16.
So
into the ground drop:
sumac, pagoda dogwood, serviceberry, witch hazel,
a bullet of longing I've been squeezing in my palm
since that hot morning you first saw me
and stopped and said,
do I know you.
How quickly a thirsty thing shoved into the wet ground will grow, will
take its place in the world, invited or no,
how shockingly fast.

17.
This endless perforation of the earth
hardens my back,
my shoulders, my thighs.
I move more now like a creature built to pounce
than be pounced.
Soon I'll be able to easily carry
the dangerous idea of my life.

18.
Today there is humidity
in the cool air.
Between the yards,
vigilant swords
of peony stalks
pierce their way skyward.
Soon small ants
will swarm
over their big pink hips,
sucking at the sweet glue
that holds them closed
and then
they will open slightly,
suddenly,
as if to breathe.
But not yet.

19.
How elastic is my heart, exactly?
How far am I willing to go to find this out?

20.
And these particular peonies
are deep pink, the color
of your lips when you've been
working in the cold
and wind.
And then you come in.

21.
A blue balloon flies low down the street
out of nowhere
and disappears.

I look all around for its source.
Pretend to myself I'm above augury.
Only I'm not.

22.
But how am I not.
How I came from poor women witchdoctors
who could poultice a rattlesnake bite
with a salve of
egg, gunpowder, salt.
And maybe save you.
How neither poverty nor sorcery can leave a woman's nerves
once she arrives at some kind of security.
How a woman never arrives at some kind of security.
How a hazel will never be just some spindly scrub
but a living pencil cup of scepters, dowsers, divining rods, wands.
And you should know—
not only does a branch of hazel steer evil someplace else.
It can unravel minatory plans already set in motion.
That trap you never intended
placed hastily in the dark.

23.
The peonies press open,
arch, their heads
expertly held, as by a lover,
so full, so heavy, so flushed;
it seems impossible
that they will ever wilt,
that they will ever go
unnoticed, unloved.

24.
One day, you pack me a lunch.
Brown paper, as if I were a girl.
But inside: flatbread,
thyme and sesame in olive oil
which, held to the light, looks
like a grass-stain in a tiny jar.
In the bottom of the bag,
a mossy cup acorn.

This was the meal that held you
when you had nothing.
You tell me this before you leave.
You leave me lunch in order to stay.

It is everything in my mouth
this wide and shapeless afternoon
as in the mouth of Krishna:
the whole universe
the history of time.

On the windowsill, I lay the acorn,
as my ancestors would.
To settle Thor and,
always in his mouth,
the threat of heat,
that unfurling tongue of lightning.

25.
I go to the woods by the river
to walk Kida. The afternoon sun
is starving.
I unhook the leash and she runs
a circular boundary around me
until she spots a herd of deer
spotting us.

She flies right into them, forces
them deep into the woods,
the white undersides of their erect tails
flash through the wild plum until
gone: the sound of hooves on dry ground and
gone: the light clatter of Kida's collar.

Leaving me. And the sound of my breath.
Surely there's a word for the kind of silence that comes
after a vanishing.
The hour a sudden diving bell
clouding with your breath.

26.
A stone in my throat.
And another word for the silence of a woman listening,
acutely, bionic,
when a thing she loves is out there.
Somewhere.
I called her name
but my call landed only feet before me
like a ball pitched by a toddler.
The woods can be like that.
Here, sound can have that sort of gravity.

I waited.
Pressed my gaze
into the darkness
between trees.

She darted out of the woods
at the exact point she had entered
and ran to me.
Mud on her hanging tongue.
A new mettle in her gait.

27.
First, we eat the foods of two different worlds.
Soon, I'd rather starve than eat
what your hands haven't made.
Wrap my arms around my middle to hide the rumble.
Only you can't hide hunger.
Who is close to you will hear your emptiness rattle around.
That low bell
in that lowly tower.

28.
Anniversaries:
the cat and I are together
six years today.

Before I found her
I had begun to decide
how to leave my life,

feeling around for a way,
dark as it was.

And here was this kitten,
half dead on the shoulder, who needed only
the heat of a body,

which I happened to have.
If little else.

The decision
lifted from me
like a balloon.
The greatest mistake a woman can make:
into the air,
into the great lung of the atmosphere.

29.
If this matter of my being,
this sentence in my invisible constitution,
unmans you, it ought.
If you're moved to back slowly away,
as from a dog bearing teeth,
you ought.
Because even as my will grows thick and leathery with time,
I remain inclined toward this edge or that.
I will always slip out from what I know
and into what I don't.

30.
You take a thousand steps my way.
You say, well, then, consider me an edge.

31.
Today the buckeye:
almond shaped leaves
now long as my hand,
a cluster of small blooms,
white with a pink shadow in the middle
out of which grows the stamen
dusted with the story of its life.

In other words, it lives.
It writhes for light now.
It shudders for rain.

I, too, will stand straight today,
long as I can.
Wear my desire like I asked for it,
like so much gold dust
to be lifted by the hindlegs of bees, to fall then from the hindlegs
into the rough hands of the wind.

32.
The days come and go.
Spring shoves the air; what I love disappears and returns.
Or not.
Low wage job, eggs in a rusting pan, an idea
that will yank me aboard as if on to a moving train,
trees not yet named, everything is here.
A ring of one's life gives way to other rings.
A long night's wandering,
that sleepless single crane.

33.
There is more of me to miss
than the animal you uncollar
in this bed.

34.
What is age
but to daily sit at your heart's piano
and practice the scales of loss?
What of yours did they pack accidently
when they left?
The father, the lover, the friend.
The name of that lake you once camped at as kids?
The secret only she had the nimbleness to hold?
An idea of who you are?
Your weird beauty?
Your specific, hidden mind?
What did they take?
What have you been asked to live without?

35.
Some weeks are fighters,
each day a fist.
I lie down
in the grass and mulch
and sunflower hulls
under the buckeye.

I am word tired.
I can't tell you what's wrong with me.
Arrows of sunlight wing through green leaves,
on to the stained knees of my work pants,
filling the stained tub
of my heart.

If I tug on this single link of sorrow,
the whole chain will move.
Desire is like this also.
But I can tell you
about desire.
I am prodigal with desire.

36.
Finally
rain.

The dogwood,
serviceberry,
coralberry
viburnum,
sumac,

every cell of the understory drunk with relief,
debauched with relief.

37.
A shock of lightning,
seen accidently,
as it usually is.
Because who can predict.

When the difference in ionic voltage
becomes too great
a balance must be struck.

It takes only a single bolt
to connect
separately charged fields. Lives.

And then comes the deep listening,
the counting.
For the reverberation.
The repercussion.
The crack.

38.
Like a rope thrown over
a branch of heaven, I can pulley myself up
out of any darkness if not any desire.
Only throw the rope.

Or at least this is what you believe.
I search for said rope.
For a time we both think
the rope is you.

39.
A small shot fired. Close.
Maybe bee-bee, or pellet.
I step out the door drying my hands on a towel.
Pete is sneaking into my backyard.
Hi Pete.
    Hi.
What are you doing, hon?
He crouches, gathers the still, grey body
of a pigeon in his little hands.

    I got this bird for my dad.
I see.
    They taste really good.
I didn't know.

40.
The rest of the dishes.
The rest of the night.
The rest of a life.

How quickly a wild thing
can meet its end and then,
as I have learned,
how delicious.

41.
Kida loves Bella,
compatriot mutt up the street.
They run together every day,
circling these small yards
like they're acres,
like they offer adequate space.
What else might they think?
All we know is all we know.

Bella and family go north for two weeks
and this morning, Kida stands atop the couch
like a billy goat, peers out the window, pants,
listens for Bella's tags.

Without the knowledge of when they'll return,
her longing is sharp

and without the knowledge that sometimes,
the beloved
never returns,
her longing is fresh, electric,

verging on joy.

42.
There is always a beloved
if you listen close to a life. Like
I know there's a thrush in this linden
or maybe in the ironwood. I know it. Know his setlist
of five songs all of which sound like R2D2
drilling See-Threepio with his impertinent questions.
Only I can't see it.
It sings and sings. Waiting for an answer or,
like R2D2,
translation to a language that is better than his.
I was saying, there is a beloved.
And between them, a singular language
forms and between them, dies.
When we leave one another,
which we will,
will the sound of us carry on?
A radio signal pulsing further and further into space?

43.
Pete and Ruthie drag
fraying lawn chairs
to the end of their porch
in order to better observe
my attempt to assemble
a manual mower
from Sears.

Their porch sits higher
than mine so the children
have loge seats
for this scene
from the day's
unrehearsed gig

which is, apparently,
a comedy. I admit
to overacting the
task, turning the parts
this way and that, pretending
to screw a wheel to my boot.
I want them to see how terrifically wrong
adults can be, and to laugh.
And to remember
this slim channel of nonsense
where our lives overlap.

44.
I take down my hair
and turn out the lamp.

At the bar down the road a band is still playing.
Sound distorts as it carries.
But this isn't why I don't sleep.

I've become hungry for a wild
I once was.
I squeeze the hunger with routines.
Make the bed.
Floss.
But even as I clean the coffee carafe
with salt, vinegar, and ice,
I'm saying under my breath,
come back.

Say when,
the wild says.
Say when.

45.
Summer lands in the middle of the week like a shotput.

And with it, a hot, hard wind.

By now, purple dame's rocket blows on the low hills along the highway.

There is in me now this small desire to run away.

There is in me now this animal eyeing the carelessly latched gate of my cage.

46.
Pete and Ruthie
(and Peter and Rosa)
have disappeared.
Three weeks now:
the shades drawn,
no car,
no movement,
no sound.

A small toy hammer,
yellow,
blows off their porch
into my yard
and I return it;
I lay it down gently,
as if it were a living thing.

47.
To stop what you do.
Push, force, run, work, eat, want, leave.
Just stop.
Is all the land asks.
It will feel
like fire to your feet at first.
But underneath your torture:
this hope chest, this dowry.

You were only ever promised to the land.

Who else has held your feet to his chest all this time?
All your life, you have only ever belonged to him.

48.
This wind.
The tallest trees of the canopy flail
wild as a tough broad losing her mind.

49.
Meanwhile, softly tucked among the great trunks,
the short lives of the understory barely move.

I wanted to be understory.
Not windbreak.
Not lightning rod.
Not this.

50.
Maybe if I leave.

Even if I don't manage to outpace me,
at least there's space in the squared backroads
of east Nebraska.
And then this giant.
I have to pull over to believe my eyes.

In the middle of nowhere, hay to the left,
corn to the right,
no other trees in sight, this cottonwood.
Taller than a church.
Thick as a grain silo.

No cottonwood should live
as long as this one,
soft as they are.
And surely it's in some farmer's way.
But it's hard to kill an old big thing.
Sentiment stops even the hardest men at times.

At least a hundred fifty years worth
of weather recorded
in its rings,
of combines, center pivot irrigators,
cab radios and the conversations
of birds apart.
The crevices in its bark are so deep, my hands
can hide in them.
I've often wanted to hide my hands,
a time out for countless small crimes.

The cottonwood leaves teeter and spin,
brush each other, hush each other.

Every single body goes to some war or another in time.
What does one do with every story,
wound, break, split,
borer, bang, cavity, scar?

Tell all who are close enough to hear:
Hush, now. Shhh.
Enough.

51.
The family returns.
Late in the night—
the click of car doors,
voices hushed, the dull yellow
porchlight, the comforting sigh
of the porchlight going out.

The next morning—
Rosa watering the lawn,
Peter gone to work,
the kids in the yard.

As if nothing had happened.
As if they'd been here all along.

52.
I'm learning to love the beast
of the world like it's a dying parent
which it is.

I'm resting my ear on its diminishing lung
so I don't miss a breath.

I'm smoothing the thick hair of its bold
foundering head.

53.
The dog won't take her eyes off the mower.
Back and forth.
She seems to wonder
just how much it can eat.
She seems to say:
be leery of those whose hunger won't be slaked.
Of him, yes.
But also of you.

54.
Sophia blows through the door,
sits at my piano,
plays badly, blows away.

Danny darts in,
borrows my blender,
returns it cleaner than he found it.

If you can't pray to the imagined gods of others,
pray to anything that makes possible
the gentler intersections of lives.

Dear House, it's me your occupant.
Please let me be a house into which any
soul may peaceably blow and unharmed, leave.
House, let them here be gods.

55.
Winds and storms barrel through
for nearly a week, lift
the earth's evidence
like a bloodhound's ears
stir the scene of the crime.

I was raised in this town.
My ghosts line the streets
as though for a parade.

Speeding ticket, first kiss, parish festival, drug deal,
Drive-in, the suicides on 50th, 49th, Miami, Walnut,
haunted house, track meet, that house we never should have entered,
bike crash, Nutcracker, car wreck.

Every day I run into a me I was once.

I don't even know how we're marking this town.
How we're planting the ghosts of ourselves
everywhere we go.

56.
Sophia, does this song you play have a name?
    I like to call it *Get Out Of My Room*.
I like it.
    I know.

Sophia runs wherever she goes.
She is barreling into her future,
barefoot.
An oak sapling is vulnerable for years,
to deer, weather, mower, tire,
until it reaches a point called *refuge age*.
If it reaches refuge age, the tree is likely
to survive, to become itself.

Yet another way
girls are not trees.

Sophia leaves fingerprints on the white keys.
I leave the piano alone for days so as not to play off
her perfect, temporary marks.

57.
I am more and more shoeless.
So as to read the land with my feet,
the particular currents of specific hungers—
water, wind, light, rest.
As between all organisms,
this pulsing grid of intersections.
But what lay under us?

The roots of a tree,
be they compression,
sinker,
or the fine hairs
of the absorbing roots,
are not designed for exposure.
They can only live
in the dark, wet secret of the land,
safe from light.

Even the understory
has an understory;
our deeply-sunk secrets
feeding us with their bone-white tongues,
we,
blind and clamoring in the light,
wet birds in a high, rickety nest.

58.
Because I love the wolf,
I know myself.

Back alone in the woods,
Kida unleashed, I see peripherally
some movement. Low.
A turkey and her fluffy
wobbly brood of chicks.

I think:
Please don't see them, Kida girl.
Please don't bolt their way.
Please, just for now, please do not be you.
Still she sees.
Still she bolts.
Still she seizes.

Still she insists on embodying
the only body she's got.

Still she loves me.
Aims to please me with this gift,
hot and limp
in her smiling jaw.

59.
I am often a fool who thinks
I'm a better animal than she.
Truly, how often do I shepherd my instincts
back into my shadow?

Peel open my jaw.
The damnatory evidence of my tongue.

60.
You leave me more and more reluctantly
but leave nonetheless.
Today, in the grass.

I'm going to let my skin dry here in this meadow on my back.
The light between dirt and canopy
shivers with pollen and cotton,

and though there's no wind against my skin,
the very top stave of the overstory sways, green
as the crabgrass poking my back.

By now, you are probably at the truck, or driving away, thinking what?

I'm thinking of how unhinged you become
with my body
when you're sad and stuck

and how I like to mistake it for desire.

And also about ascension.
How this tree pulls water from its roots
all the way up to the third story of its body?
The tip of the leaf you can't even see from here?

It's not capillarity.
The way molecules of water creep
slowly up the hidden, narrow conduits of an organism.

Nor is it the pressure of one's atmosphere.
Or the pressure of one's roots.

Nourishment defies gravity, climbs, by way of transpirational pull.
One molecule after another evaporating from a leaf,
vanishing and vanishing so dependably,
the next one in line appears to be pulled
into place.
By the vanishing.

What mechanism does not have loss built in?
If I lie here alone until darkness comes,
what animal will your absence call in?

61.
To love entire
is to lose entire.
First, I think: I was no one anyway.
Then, I think: But I'm all I have.

62.
Maybe if I retract, pull
into the warm self of myself
like a claw.

Only I'm more container
than claw, aren't I?
What is poured in
will cause a pouring out someplace else,
won't it.

63.
My sister marries on an island far away.
The whole tribe lifts from the middle of America
to fly down, pale migratory birds,

to where patrons of an outdoor bar applaud the sunsets.
Where I lean on the fat body of a baobob tree.
Where rains drop suddenly out of the bright blue air
like sunlit confetti.

On the beach, the bare legs of women fill me with tenderness.
I want to cradle those soft limbs and say,
I see the weight she makes you carry.
I see the monsters she has freed
on the field of her heart,
how they trample and gnaw and deplete.
I see how they've tripled your load.

64.
Come evening, the family circles in the sand
to sing, pray, invoke
the animal of marriage.

The animal of marriage
glides into the circle
light and perfect as a dancer.

She shimmers so beautifully we weep.

We don't even notice
the little hitch in her hip.

We can't even fathom how she'll cripple in time.

65.
The sand is day-warm beneath our feet.
Unless you burrow, as I do now.
Unless you're hopelessly sucked
into the wet and dark beneath all warm things,
that soft bed littered
with the turned particles of the dead.

66.
I fall into my home like it has arms.
I love my threadbare blanket. I love the sound of my body alone
and occasionally, the measured tic of claws across a worn floor.
I love that sometimes, one can just be.
One can mean nothing.

67.
South of the city is a sixty acre stretch of land
rugged and strange and small enough
to have been left alone by progress.
In its center is a bur oak
hundreds of years old.
I visit it,
old bitch of a tree.
I need to sit on its knobby flare
for a moment,
lean against her ragged bark.
My spine requires
bolstering,
a good talking to.
A reminder of how to quit a thing
and stay quit.

I came here first with you.
Here we were once watched
by a camouflaged hunter
in a deer stand.
Here Kida once lept into a pond
covered with a bright carpet of duckweed,
mistaking it for solid ground.

She came home smelling of pond.
I came home smelling of you.

Now I come alone.

Then I'll never come again.

68.
But I don't know that yet.
I do know this: the name of the butterflies
so abundant in here.
Clouded Sulfurs—
winged and yellow thumbprints
among the partridge pea
and ironweed.

They will live a single month.
All of their firsts and lasts
will happen right here.

I too would fly.

69.
From them I remember
there are lives of mine
being lived without me.
They hum
in the shadows, run
on the idea of me

alone.
Likewise

they have become
the hindwing of my mind,
intricately marked,
fashioned for steerage,
like a rudder.

70.
Occasionally, a clearing.
That absence before the process
of succession.
After a clearing—
the brush fire, the clear cut—
first come the tough plants,
made for barren space, bare sun.
Then come the
grasses, shrubs, trees,
then canopy, understory,
forest.

In theory, succession peaks, completes.
The habitat now stable.
The truth being that,
more often than not,
a stable state
is never reached.

71.
Past the oak,
a small hill
covered
with Queen Anne's lace.
It's chest-high,
a thin, light green
and feels
like a child's hair
against the skin.
I am seduced now by every last
habitative element
that has homed us in any way,
gave us shade in which to eat our lunch,
or a trunk tough enough to brace us.

The clover-scented air lifts from an unmowed ditch along the highway,
floats through my window,
and I'm no longer a woman
driving to work
but a bit player in the endlessly driving penetrations
of the continuing world.

I have to stop.
I have to close my eyes.
I have to stop.

72.
One story will always replace another in time.
Habitat formation gives way
to habitat fragmentation.
The way we break and we break and we break,
we live apart and apart,
wedged between us:
progress,
shame.

The greater the fragmentation,
the weaker the habitat.
We are shatter,
we are scatter,
we are starve.

73.
Back home, back in the yard,
under the wings of the buckeye's longer limbs
the young serviceberry tree
blooms boldly,
yields berries
of a taut, pale green.

The robins and I
eye them
with a common, primal

patience
waiting

for the quick turn to red
then purple,

for the pressing outward
of the thin flesh,
changed,

for its quiet sweetness
in the mouth,

its mysterious seed,
soft between the teeth,
or beak.

74.
An idea comes.
A glimpse of myself on the other side
of this tangled, impossible love.
Where I am weathered and awake.
Where my body is a monster
patchworked from history,
from every resistance
and every yield,
visible seams that trace
the hemorrhages of grief.
Well-oiled zippers of my doings
and my undoings,
working still.

Where I walk my monster
proudly through the days.
Where nights I find a few to love it
as good and hard as I.

75.
A new baby arrives in the tribe.
She throws light, kaleidoscopic,
across the meanest hours,
changing them. Me.

My bones can't even hold the love together.

I leave my diaphragm in a drawer for two months.
I vibrate in the eye of a perfect storm of chemicals, loneliness, love.
I suddenly want an accident
of the farthest reaching sort.
And if I could admit,
a love that doesn't leave.

This is not to be.

The storm uncurls its hand and drops me.

But once, on the street,
I saw a boy I thought should have come from me
but found a better course.
I smiled at him. He looked away.

76.
Less and less light
makes its way
through the bee tree's canopy.
What was a soft rain of sun
weeks ago is now
just an occasional diagonal,
shaking with purpose,
quick to disappear.

Its sweet white flowers
curl, brown, fall,
cover the sidewalk
with their soft gold flesh.

I walk shoeless through it,
wandering, in the middle
of a bruising night.
I track tree droppings
through the house
and back into my bed.

You will smell it there.
You will know where I have been.

77.
Get out of my room.

78.
In the morning I pass a redbud up the street
that has distorted itself entirely
in order to get light.

It lives under an enormous silver maple
and is shaped
now
like a vertical fan
or a hand
open for something
that does not come.

79.
I didn't want to see that.

80.
Why must my soul
insist on holding the past to her breast?

And not just the babes of sweeter, gone hours,
but the sharp-toothed, the brutal, the sick.
All have their turn at latch.

Even this day—
full of enough rage
to send my fist into a plaster wall—
even for this
she will one day unfasten
her old, soft shirt.

81.
In a tent by the river:
the light through its thin walls—red,
the sky through a split seam—blue,
my pain—red,
your body, when I'm done with it—red,
in places—blue.

82.
This is the brown thrasher
in a hazelnut field:
kettle kettle kettle,
itch, itch,
true low, true low.

There are so many songs to sing,
where does one begin?
So many occasions to,
as the soprano put it,
control the scream.

Even the crow of the heart
does not come unaccompanied.

Away away,
away away.

And when the crow quits,
it cocks its head and listens.
It's hearing me,
years from now,
never having left this place,
some part of me still sweat bound
and starving
in a numbered room.

83.
By August
the days swell beyond capacity
and, by afternoon, deflate.
All the organisms,
overstretched, overwrought,
wilt.

84.
The month's knuckles turn white.
The understory clutched and struggling.
I wonder what it would take to walk away.

85.
Elsewhere, the mountains, oceans,
islands, seas—daydreams
of the flatlanders—
startle and pierce. Snowbind. Saturate.

Could I live
with beauty that mean?
Can one every truly leave?

Here is a moment of intolerable loss,
or teardown of the single great love,
and no matter how far or long you go,
you will fold back to these
like a book closes on itself.

86.
I feel a restless night ahead
before I even clock out.
Heading home on the highway, windows down,
there is, now literally, smoke on the air.
Why not drive toward its plume,
pyrocumulous,
all the way to the river.

On the Iowa side—at least
a hundred cottonwoods in flames.
Most were dead from the flood but standing, still,
bark shed, fat white candles
on the cake of the bank.

From a distance, fires appear to throb.
I park near the Mormon Bridge,
a steel and concrete replacement of the one
my ancestors once crossed
hot on the trail of a brand new god.

87.
Prescribed burn,
chucked cigarette,
carelessly snuffed campfire.
All possible. None unusual.

Come night, a full moon rises like a hot brain.
Bone planet above mile fire,
showdown of the light thieves.

88.
And then, the flame hops
the water.
Jumps states.
I think I'm too old not to know
that a fire can leap a river like a cat.

An old timer, face lit orange like mine,
tells me through cigarette-bit teeth
that it was a controlled burn got away from them.
A man outta know what he's doing,
he adds.

89.
Back home, it's hard to sleep.
I still feel the heat on my skin.

Have you ever prescribed a fire for your life's virus?
Or for its excess? Or for its weakness?
A minor fire.
Boundaries clear.
Containment guaranteed.

Did you then unchain a hell wild enough
to clear a river?
To eat a valley of trees
casually
as fish sticks from a tray
before your favorite show?

90.
We enter a heat so still it feels
like the planet quit. A final cog caught
in its eternal wheel.
Too hot, too done to even say,
it was fun. Night everyone.

I never know when or if you'll come.

91.
Flies, mosquitos, birds,
all the winged things travel slowly now.
My own wings,
wet and frayed,
no longer lift me.
There will be no more hovering
above you now, electric,
impossibly light.

92.
After two weeks of heat,
stillness is our last resort
and only pardon.
I retreat to the shade of my house,
of my life,
to the deeper shade of myself
and I wait.
What freedom in knowing there is nothing left to do.

93.
The understory is growing up,
is sinking deep into place.
When did I abandon the idea of casting out?
I could travel the country of this yard all my life
and never fully know it.
Same goes for this body.
Same goes for this love.

94.
How little it takes, sometimes.
How much.
How hard to know which.
The shortening days,
how hard the shrinking light will work, how far it will go
to put its fading mouth to the back of your neck.

95.
Is the self dark matter?
Entirely unknowable
but for its gravity,
but for the fact of its being
pulled and pulled
and tirelessly pulled?

96.
Early morning. The sky fills with grey light and then
darkens again like
the sun just up and changed its mind.
Storm light electrifies
the green leaves and rain
blackens the bark.
These are the colors that rush the house
like holy men to the possessed.
For one sweet morning my hunger
finds some company in this green burning breeze,
this blackening rain but,

a punch clock waits
for a card with my name,
the little dots saying I was here,
how I came and went,
just how long I stayed.

97.
The palms of my hands miss you.
And the back of my tongue.
And the arches of my feet.
And also my toes.
The back of my neck misses you.
And my one turned vertebra.
My hips.
My scars.
My ears.
Where I am soft.
Where I am hard.
Everywhere you rested.
Everywhere you woke.

98.
My friend in the learning hospital says that a bullet
doesn't just enter the body and stop.
It bounces, she says, as if you were to throw a rubber ball
in a small room
as hard as you could. She points
to the ceiling, the wall, the table, the floor.

Why are you telling me this?

There's just too much to know, she says.

For days, storms spin and rip
the tedious weave of the city.
The leader of a sycamore cracks,
steps on the neighbor's sedan
like a paper crane.
It feels like a relief.
The sky throwing the fit I cannot,
tearing the shirt I cannot,
pulling up trees like a god.

99.
A new morning, cool air,
repentant sky.
The witchhazel's leaves sway slowly,
carefully, an old woman
shaking her yellow head, again
disappointed in some small way.

The pagoda dogwood, whose branches are always raised
in a way that seems to ask why,
sags as though weighted.

The whole understory moves like this
as if recovering from a terrible blow
or a beauty that can't be known again.

It is the morning after the graduation,
the wedding, the consummation,
the party, the accident, the concert,
the funeral, the dance.
We expect to wake up changed
but all throughout the air—
the sadness and relief
that we have not.

100.
After the upheaval,
even of the sort we think we want,
especially then,
how we look longingly on monotony,
picking up the pieces
of our feral eruptions.

The understory is quiet,
ready to return
to its everyday hungers—
light,
water,
oxygen,
root.

101.
The bee tree begins to lose its leaves—
brown serrated hearts
spin to the ground.

This organism has a thousand hearts to drop,
on to the lawn and to the neighbors,
down the sidewalk and streets,
on the wind and behind, beyond, and into
all the little nowheres that surround our lives,
the corners, the gutters, the underneaths, the maybes.

Everywhere are the pieces of us, flying and buried and disappearing,
barely, and also unbearably,
missed.

102.
The sweet smell of decomposing leaves
someplace close.
Halloween and brush fires.
The kids play late as possible
because the smell tells them
winter is close and soon
they will have to take their brave little lives
inside,
into the vast, unknowable territory
of their homes.

103.
It's startling how quickly life leaves—
the understory's hasty surrender.
Soft tissue contracts, browns,
bends in on itself as if in an effort
to disappear entirely.

104.
Pete joins me in the yard
with his miniature rake. He doesn't watch
what he's doing but studies me.
I am, perhaps, the object of a six year old's love.
Neither of us knows exactly how to be.
Do we speak? Would it be unkind to look him
in the eyes? I admire his industry aloud.
I tell him the names of things
as I was told. And because it's what I hold on to now,
the names of what I know,
in the face of all I don't.
Buckeye, I say. Dogwood. These twisty things are sumac.
That's a serviceberry.
ser-vice-ber-ry, he repeats.
It used to be, when the serviceberry fruited,
folks knew the ground had thawed enough
to bury their dead. The ones who died over winter.
And hold services for them.
So, serviceberry.

I've not mastered the art of telling little.
You could say I'm likely to overstory a thing.
Pete studies the serviceberry. Rakes slowly,
his mind moving now in an elsewhere of long ago.
The same fruiting tree as this,
the same bodies finally put to rest.

105.
Prickly white frost on brown leaves,
cold white dust on the grass,
our breath in clouds.

106.
How quickly we forget a hot breeze
over bare bodies
in stiff crabgrass, so green it seems
like the blood of green.
And the cicadas when the light lows.
And that place where the edge of a fence panel
is curling up and animals
are coming and going in the dark.

107.
Somewhere
the coming cold builds momentum,
arrives fully formed.
The air is full of small pins,
microscopic to the skin and lungs.
Entire cross sections of my body, my heart,
having been asleep,
are perforated and wake.
This house
has a hundred seams where the cold sneaks in.

I won't look for heat anywhere but your mouth.

108.
Some days I hope
for my best.
Some days to stay just this side
of unforgivable.

109.
The cold drops deeper.
It seems to have wrapped around my bones.
It's either trying to reset them
or crush them.

110.
I drive to the river after work,
night already shoving in even though it's afternoon.

Last month the river was a song,
but now it's a lecture with slides.
According to the river,
whole wings of a body can freeze

so much so that this currenting thing
appears not to move.

Still, the river's lecture is long and full
of contradictions.

111.
The remaining daylight
throws up her hands and leaves.
Now the river's saying something
about how you can never be you again,
as you were.
That, depending on the slope gradient,
channel roughness,
tides,
you flow, you turn yourself over,
at about two miles an hour.
But—
your direction never changes.
One could say,
she adds,
that you are never you and always you
at the same time.

112.
She would like to add one more salient point.
But it's four degrees and dropping.
The river's breath is ragged now,
her voice hoarse.

The organ of my skin is so cold
it burns.
Bad as a planet betrayed
by its own.

113.
I have hated numbers
for all they leave out
and here I stand against my nature,
wanting for an extracting of the unknowns,
to solve for x,
to balance either side of the equation.
The brutal algebra of the end.

114.
We are saved by light wind, by turns
in the atmospheric tides, by the ever-fraying cord
between giving up and stupid hope, by touch
and by not touching, we are saved
by our violent desire and then by the abandoning
of it so we can breathe, so we can breathe,
so that we can please god breathe.

115.
What are we now but the accumulation of lightness?
The slightest beauty unravels us,
too heavy to look for long or lift.
I avert my eyes from your eyes and also
from the clearing sky,
its clouds plump and golden, receding,
and from the thin rim of snow on every last branch,
and from the blue light of evening turning
the snow blue
and also from the moon,
pouring its pearly sorrow down into
the bare canopies of the buckeye and the bee tree
and spilling over as it always does.
It always does and I can't look.
I just can't look anymore.
My heart.

116.
I poured all I can't hold
on to the land. The overflow. As we all do.
The land continues to hold me
and it continues to hold all the selves I'm too weak to be.
Where do you think it all goes?
The idea you didn't have the courage to say
until it was too late.
The hunger you wouldn't unloose
because you thought your body unworthy.
Every weird, bold move you aborted,
sucked out of you before it could speak for itself.
Where did you think it all goes?

117.
The grey land and grey sky pour into one another
their dark moods.

Every winter feels differently permanent.

I rush down a sidewalk, pushing all the while against my desire
to be alone with your absence.
I am expected. And I'm late.

What makes me turn my head of a sudden to see you sitting in a
    window,
seeing me, your breath visible against the glass, mine visible against
    the air.

How long do I stand there and more, how on earth do my legs go
    forward,
toward a restaurant, where glass and forgetting and laughter
clatter in the warm, yeasty air.

I don't know if my throat is closing around the cold
or the desire not to cry
or around the desire for your rough hand
wrapped lightly around my neck like a scarf
like love.

118.
Still, I will come to you again and again
before this is over for good. There will be a last time
for us. We will take ourselves off like winter coats
and slip together into the gap
between time and history. There we will be
heat, rain, light alone.
Invisible communion of organisms.
After that day, we will be only a shiver in my brain,
a story pulsing in the slighter branches of the understory
while they reach and reach for whatever
available light.

119.
A snow day. A small unpaid liberation.
The old fireplace lets more smoke into the white air
than it does the house.
No job will wear you out so hard as grief.
What is crucial, what remains, is being squeezed from what is
    transient,
what must, by design, leave.
How else could it be. It will stop just this side of crushing you.

You will breathe differently then, having been broke
and left alive, the sky in a quiet collapse,
a fire not far from your feet.

120.
The snow goes on impossibly
like a shy person
suddenly unable to stop talking.

By evening,
there are drifts up to my hip.
I lift in layers,
from the top down,
its radiant weight.

www.ingramcontent.com/pod-product-compliance
Lightning Source LLC
Chambersburg PA
CBHW030200100526
44592CB00009B/380